1st Make a place in your home where you will think about Advent

Make it special by putting your Advent calendar, candle, crib-set, or wreath there.

2nd Find a jar or pot and decorate it if you like

Use it to collect coins through Advent and then give them to a charity.

3rd Think back over the last year

What made you most happy? Thank God for this.

1st Sunday of Advent

On the First Sunday of Advent we remember people in the Old Testament like Abraham and Sarah, Moses and Miriam, David and Solomon. We call them Patriarchs – the mothers and fathers of our faith – the people who first responded to God's call.

The Lord said to Abram, "Leave your land, your family, and your father's household for the land that I will show you. I will make of you a great nation and will bless you. I will make your name respected, and you will be a blessing. I will bless those who bless you, those who curse you I will curse; all the families of the earth will be blessed because of you."
Genesis 12:1–3

Pray

God of Abraham and Sarah,
You gave them faith to listen when you spoke, and strength to go where you sent them.
Help us to make room in our lives to hear your loving call and be ready to respond.
Amen.

4th Clear out a room, a cupboard or a shelf

Give away as much of it as you can.

5th Take time to think of someone who has been important to you this year

Tell them in a Christmas card why they mean so much to you.

6th Look carefully at a piece of holly or at a pine cone

Take time to notice its shape, its texture and its colors.

7th Buy some food and give it to your local food bank ☆

8th Take time out and do something really nice that you have wanted to do for a long time ☆

9th Think of someone you wouldn't ☆ usually buy a present for (and who may not buy you one)

Give them something you think they would really like.

10th Feed the birds ☆

Maybe make a fat ball (see recipe on the website).

2nd Sunday of Advent

On the Second Sunday of Advent we remember the prophets, people like Elijah, Isaiah, and Micah. They listened to God's call and pointed others to what God had to say.

The royal line of David is like a tree that has been cut down; but just as new branches sprout from a stump, so a new king will arise from among David's descendants. The spirit of the LORD will give him wisdom and the knowledge and skill to rule his people. He will know the LORD's will and honor him, and find pleasure in obeying him.
Isaiah 11:1–3a (GNB)

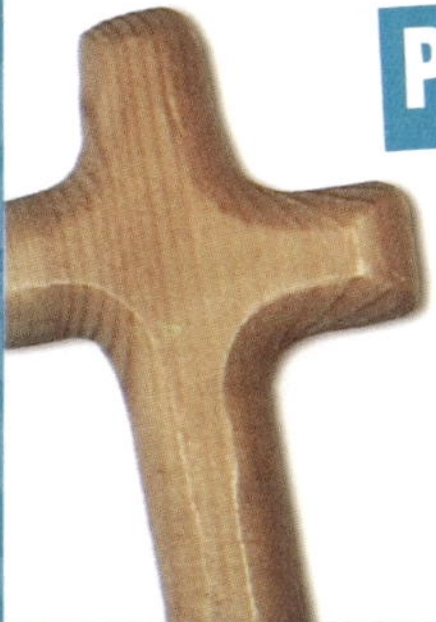

Pray

God of Elijah, Isaiah, and Micah,
You gave them courage
to speak your words of hope.
Help us to make room in our lives for your love and peace to grow. Amen.

11th Make (or buy) a Christmas decoration and give it to someone ☆

(See suggestions on the website.)

12th What is your favorite Christmas carol? ☆

Find the words to it, read them slowly and think about what it says (you can sing it too if you like!).

13th Plant some bulbs inside or outside, ready for the spring ☆

14th What do you wish for the world? Write a prayer saying what you hope for

You could write it on a decorated piece of paper and hang it on the Christmas tree.

15th Write a poem or draw a picture that says something about what Christmas means to you

16th Think of someone who is very busy at this time of year

Offer to do something to help them.

17th Turn off the lights

Sit in darkness for a few minutes. What does it feel like?

3rd Sunday of Advent

On the Third Sunday of Advent
we remember John the Baptist,
who told everyone
to prepare for Jesus.

The beginning of the good news about Jesus Christ, God's Son, happened just as it was written about in the prophecy of Isaiah:

Look, I am sending my messenger before you. He will prepare your way, a voice shouting in the wilderness: "Prepare the way for the Lord; make his paths straight."

John the Baptist was in the wilderness calling for people to be baptized to show that they were changing their hearts and lives and wanted God to forgive their sins.
Mark 1:1–4

Pray

God of John the Baptist,
You sent him to prepare people
to welcome Jesus, your Son.
Help us to make room in our lives
that we might be ready to
welcome him this Christmas.
Amen.

18th

Make (or buy) some mince pies or Christmas cookies and give them to someone to say thank you for who they are ☆

19th

Take time to ☆ watch one of your favorite Christmas videos

Invite someone special to watch it with you.

20th

Watch (but don't touch) a candle flame ☆

What colors can you see in it? How does it make you feel?

21st

Go for a walk ☆

Make time to notice what you pass. What colors can you see and what sounds can you hear?

22nd Think back over the last year

What do you need to say sorry for, or to let go of before Christmas? Give it to God.

23rd Find someone older than you and ask them what Christmas was like when they were a child

24th As you make your final preparations for Christmas,

hanging up your stockings, or putting presents under the tree,

take a moment to thank God for what God has already given you

4th Sunday of Advent

On the Fourth Sunday of Advent we remember Mary, the mother of Jesus, who waited for his birth just like we are waiting now.

The angel said, "Don't be afraid, Mary. God is honouring you. Look! You will conceive and give birth to a son, and you will name him Jesus. He will be great and he will be called the Son of the Most High. The Lord God will give him the throne of David his father. He will rule over Jacob's house forever, and there will be no end to his kingdom." **Luke 1:30–33**

Pray

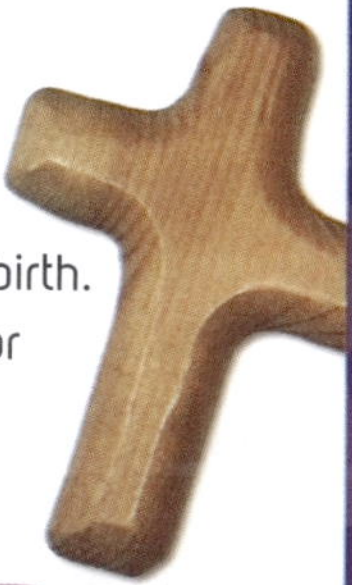

God of Mary, You gave her the patience to wait with hope for your birth. Help us to make room in our lives for your joy as we wait for Christmas. Amen.

Christmas Day!

Today is Christmas Day. It's time to celebrate the birth of Jesus!

Take a few minutes today to read **Luke 2:6–7**, to pray the prayer and to thank God for Christmas.

Pray

God of all joy,
You gave your Son to us at the first Christmas.
Help us to make room for him in our lives
today and every day.
Amen.